Why does a battery make it go?

Jackie Holderness

Aladdin/Watts
London • Sydney

Why does a battery make it go?

Today is Zack's birthday. His friends have come to his party. The children are having fun. Amy, Jo and Steve are dancing to the CD player.

Can we take the CD player outside?

Doesn't it need electricity to make it work? There are no sockets outside.

Let's see how the children find out.

Electricity gives the CD player energy to light up, spin the CD and make sounds.

If you plug the CD player in and switch it on electricity flows along the lead.

1

Those batteries are too small. These are the right size.

Dad says we need four batteries to make it work without a lead.

2

4

We need to match the + and - signs on the batteries with the + and - signs on the machine.

3

It works! Batteries provide electricity as well. But you must put them in the right way.

4

Why it works

When you plug a machine into a wall socket and switch it on, electricity from the socket gives it energy to move or make light, sound or heat. This electricity comes into your home from a power station. Chemicals inside a battery also make electricity. But you must match up the plus signs (+) and the minus signs (-) on the battery with the signs inside the machine so the electricity can flow.

Solve the puzzle!

Which machines use electricity in your house? Write down a list, or make a chart of machines like the one on page 22.

How does electricity work?

Now it's time for Zack to open his presents. Amy's present is a lamp. Zack's mum plugs it into the wall. Steve's present to Zack is a toy robot. Zack is putting batteries into its back to make it work.

Lots of my presents use electricity. But how does electricity work?

7

SAFETY FIRST!

NEVER touch a light bulb which has just been switched off! Always make sure it has cooled down first!

Let's see how the children find out.

Let's try a second bulb. I'll connect it here so it still makes a loop.

That works too! So the wires must make a loop for the electricity to flow.

Electricity only flows in a loop. Here the battery, wires and bulb make a loop, or circuit. The battery makes electricity flow along the wire to the bulb, then back to the battery along the other wire. Two or more bulbs can be connected to one battery, but the wires must always make a circuit. In a house, the lights are connected by one or more circuits.

Solve the puzzle

What happens when you try lighting two bulbs? Make a circuit using two bulbs. Are they as bright as one bulb on its own? **9**

What do switch is do?

It's time for Zack's birthday cake. He takes a big breath to blow out all the candles with one big puff! Everyone is ready to sing "Happy Birthday".

Let's see how the children find out.

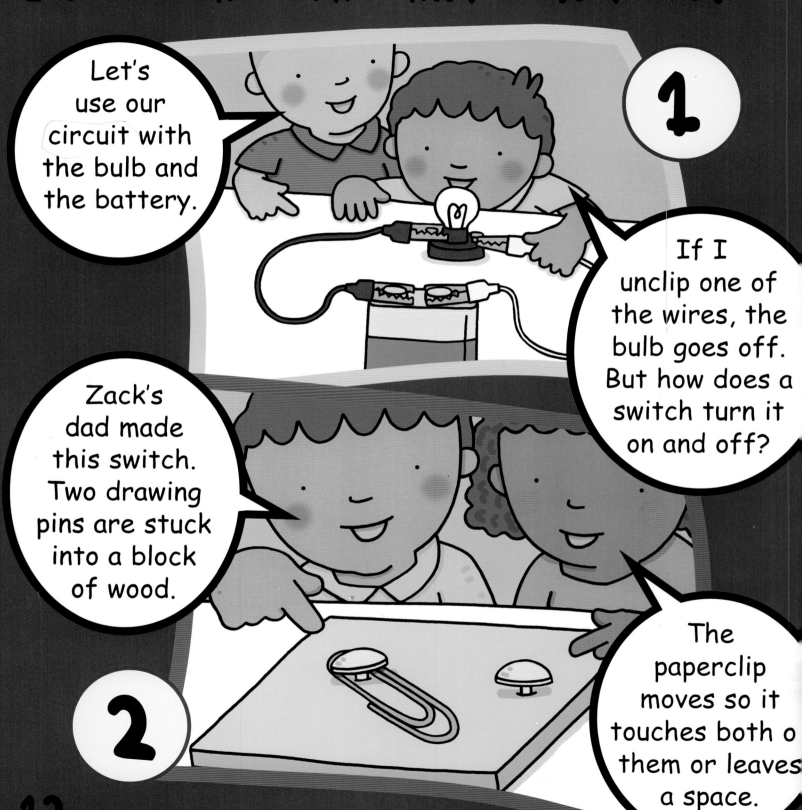

> Let's add the switch to the circuit. When the paperclip touches both drawing pins, the bulb glows.

3

4

> But if I swing the paperclip away, we make a break in the circuit and the bulb goes out.

Why it works

When Jo moves the paperclip, she makes a break in the circuit and the bulb goes out. If there is a break in any circuit, the electricity cannot flow around in a loop, so it does not flow at all. Most switches have a piece of metal that moves like the paperclip, so the circuit can be broken or connected.

Solve the puzzle

Which metals make good switches? Try using coins, a fork, a gold or silver ring or a strip of metal kitchen foil. Use a simple circuit with a bulb and battery.

Why are wires covered in plastic?

The next day, the children go to play in Steve's garden. Steve's dad has been mowing the lawn with an electric mower. Now he is winding up its long lead, which had been plugged into a socket inside the house.

Why do electric wires and leads have plastic on the outside?

14

15

I'll try this metal spoon. Now the bulb is glowing again!

3

So electricity flows along the metal parts of a lead, but the plastic must stop it from flowing anywhere else.

Electricity flows easily along some materials. We call them conductors. Many metals are very good conductors, so they are used in electric wires. Other materials, like plastic, stop the flow of electricity. They are called insulators. Plastic is used to cover metal wires so electricity can't flow out and harm you.

Solve the puzzle

Why do you think it's very dangerous to touch anything electric with wet hands? Think about whether electricity can flow through water.

17

How can electricity make a magnet?

The children are playing inside. Amy is doing some experiments with a set of magnets and the boys are playing with Steve's toy crane.

19

We need a piece of wire about twice as long as I am. Mum said we should wrap it around this long steel nail.

1

I've left some wire loose at each end, so we can fix the ends to the battery.

2

Let's see if it works like a magnet. We can test it with these metal paperclips.

20

A wire works like a magnet when electricity flows through it. Its magnetic strength can be increased by wrapping it around an iron nail. When you turn off the electricity, the magnet stops working. The magnetic effect of electricity can also be used to make motors turn in washing machines, fans and even cars.

Solve the puzzle

How can you test the power of a battery? Make a magnet like Steve's and connect it to different types of battery. See which one picks up the most paperclips.

21

Did you solve the puzzle?

Which machines use electricity in your house?

You can probably find lots of machines that use electricity in your house. But be careful what you touch! Can you make a chart showing machines that use electricity from a socket and those which use batteries?

Electricity from socket	Electricity from battery
Lamp	Torch
Freezer	Watch
Cooker	Camera
Hairdryer	Car lights
Television	Mobile phone
CD player	CD player

What happens when you try lighting two bulbs?

Two light bulbs in a simple circuit with one battery (above) don't shine as brightly as one bulb on its own. But see how bright they are if you arrange the bulbs and battery in a circuit like the one below.

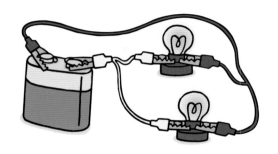

Which metals make good switches?

Most do. Electricity flows easily through metals such as iron, brass, copper, silver and aluminium, so they are good conductors. Copper is often used to make electrical wires.

How can you test the power of a battery?

The battery that makes the magnet pick up the most paperclips is giving the magnet the most power. If you add an extra battery to the circuit, does the magnet pick up even more paperclips?

Why is it dangerous to touch anything electric with wet hands?

Electricity flows easily through water, so if your hands get wet (like Amy on page 15), be careful not to touch any electric plugs or machines. The electricity flowing through them could flow into your body and hurt or even kill you.

Index

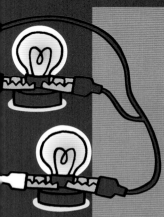

© Aladdin Books Ltd 2002

Designed and produced by
Aladdin Books Ltd
28 Percy Street
London W1T 2BZ

First published in
Great Britain in 2002 by
Franklin Watts
96 Leonard Street
London EC2A 4XD

ISBN 0 7496 4744 2

A catalogue record for this book is
available from the British Library.

Printed in U.A.E.
All rights reserved

Editor
Jim Pipe

Science Consultants
Helen Wilson and David Coates
Westminster Institute of Education
Oxford Brookes University

Science Tester
Alex Laar

Design
Flick, Book Design and Graphics

Illustration
Jo Moore